SKITS BLITZ

CORMAC G. MCDERMOTT BA MEconSc

Order this book online at www.trafford.com
or email orders@trafford.com

Most Trafford titles are also available at major online book retailers.

Printed in the United States of America.

ISBN: 978-1-4907-2156-9 (sc)
ISBN: 978-1-4907-2157-6 (e)

Trafford rev. 01/06/2014

 www.trafford.com

North America & international
toll-free: 1 888 232 4444 (USA & Canada)
fax: 812 355 4082

CONTENTS

CHAPTER 1:

Comedy Sketches

**SCENE FROM A BAR ON THE SOUTH SIDE OF DUBLIN—
SHAUNA SEES A GUY SHE LIKES AND DECIDES TO FLIRT WITH
HIM.**

SHAUNA: 'Hi. I'm Shauna. What's your name?'

GUY: 'Hi. My name is Jamie'.

SHAUNA: 'Where are you from and what do you work at?'

JAMIE: 'I live in Blackrock and work for a conservatory conversions company. Where are you from?'

SHAUNA: 'Donnybrook. Conservatory conversions, ey? Does that mean I have to take up rugby if I would like you to do a job for me then?'

JAMIE: 'Donnybrook. Very nice. What do you mean about taking up rugby?'

SHAUNA: 'Well, if I don't score a try, I have no chance of getting an attempt at a 'conversion', do I?'!

JAMIE: 'Oh right, I see what you mean. That's very clever. You seem to be bright. Are you a university student or something?'

SHAUNA: 'I actually just graduated with a master's degree in law from University College, Dublin only a few months back. Why don't you give me your number and I'll give you a call some time'.

JAMIE: 'Sure. That sounds cool. Can I buy you a cocktail?'

SHAUNA: 'No, please let me buy you one'!

THE YOUNG COUPLE CONTINUE TO TALK AND LEARN MORE ABOUT EACH OTHER.

SCENE FROM A BAR ON THE NORTH SIDE OF DUBLIN—A GROUP OF MEN IN THEIR FORTIES ARE WATCHING THE REPUBLIC OF IRELAND PLAY AN INTERNATIONAL SOCCER GAME.

JACKO: 'That was a bad result for us, ey?'

NEZ: 'Yeah. With that group of players it looks like we may not qualify for a major tournament for quite some time'.

WALSHER: 'So much for that 'You'll Never Beat The Irish' nonsense'.

CHARLIE: 'The only way you wouldn't 'beat' the Irish these days is if you sent eleven boiled eggs in green jerseys out onto that pitch'!

IT TAKES A WHILE FOR THE QUIP TO REGISTER WITH THE LADS BUT THEY ALL CHUCKLE AND AGREE WHEN IT DOES.

Cormac G. McDermott BA MEconSc

SCENE FROM AN INTERNET FORUM—A BIT OF BANTER IS FLOWING BETWEEN SOME FOOTBALL FANS.

BILLY BOY: 'Enjoy winning the league while you can, Tim. We'll be back before long'.

TIM: 'Enjoying winning the league in a canter is something all us Taigs are revelling in, Billy Boy'.

BILLY BOY: 'When we get back in the top flight there'll be a better chance of you seeing a blue moon than watching your captain lifting trophies again'!

TIM: 'If I was interested in seeing a blue 'moon', I'd check out the reflection of my ass after I'd sat in a freezer for a few hours'!

BILLY BOY: 'Very funny, Tim! You lot have no regard for the union either, do you?'

TIM: 'We have total regard for union. The fact that we would rather that spiritual union is something you people find empowering into being problematic, totally self-interested only while showing a united materialistically-orientated front of power-playing against vulnerable people'!

BILLY BOY: 'What are you on about you lunatic?'!

TIM: 'There you go referring to moons again, Silly Boy! If you people were to participate in Eucharistic Adoration, you would be self-renderingly amplified discernment-ees'!

BILLY BOY: 'Goodness me. Where did that come from you freak?'!

BOTH MEN CONTINUE TO FIRE OPINIONS BACK AND FORTH.

SCENE FROM A BARBER SHOP—OSCAR IS SITTING DOWN AND WAITING FOR HIS TURN TO HAVE HIS HAIR CUT. HIS FRIEND, PETE, WALKS IN AND THEY BEGIN TO CHAT AND CATCH UP.

OSCAR: 'Alright Pete. How are things? Haven't seen you in a while'.

PETE: 'Hi Oscar. I'm grand thanks. Yeah, it's been a while. Not much going on with me. Are you still living beside that eejit Tom Feely?'

OSCAR: 'I am. He's a bit of a gobsh*te alright. I tell you with the way we are talking about him it's a good thing his first name isn't Touchy, ey?!'

PETE: 'H'har har, Oscar. That's pretty funny mate. By the way, does Brian Nick still live the other side of you? He's a good guy'.

OSCAR: 'He does'.

PETE: 'His brother has been in and out of the cracker factory on a regular basis over the last twenty years, hasn't he? What's his name again, I can't think of it?'

OSCAR: 'I think you may be referring to A Few Sandwiches Short Of A Pick, right?!'

THE TWO MEN BURST OUT LAUGHING AND CONTINUE ON WITH THEIR CONVERSATION.

SCENE FROM A PARK—TWO PALS, PACKIE AND STEVE, ARE OUT ON A WALK. STEVE IS A CHARACTER AND DECIDES HE IS GOING TO HUMOUR HIS MATE.

STEVE: 'Hey Packie. Do you know Paul Fleming from The Grove Estate?'

PACKIE: 'Yeah. He was a few years behind me when I was in secondary school. Why do you ask?'

STEVE: 'I was talking to Francesca Perkins a while ago and she said that after he slept with her it was a case of him losing his virginity. She was very surprised as she thinks he is a really nice guy and is quite handsome'.

PACKIE: 'Francesca Perkins? I heard she's a bleedin' animal in the scratcher'!

STEVE: 'True. She told me she sunk her teeth into both of his ears as they were reaching climax'!

PACKIE: 'I'd say that was a real shock for Paul, ey?'

STEVE: 'Indeed. 'Once shy, twice bitten', right?'

PACKIE: 'Ha ha. That's gas buddy. I must tell that to the missus'.

SCENE FROM A BUILDING SITE—LEO AND TOM ARE ON THEIR BREAK.

LEO: 'I tell ya, Tom, the foreman is very slow on the uptake. Do you not think he's a bit thick?'

TOM: 'I've been thinking that myself. This job should be a piece of p*ss but he's organising things all the wrong way, ey?'

LEO: 'I know I got an average Leaving Cert but I can safely say the man is intellectually challenged mate'.

TOM: 'Yeah, he's as thick as the planks that were used to put that roof up'!

LEO: 'Are you joking? He's even thicker than the planks used to build Noah's submarine'!

TOM: 'That's pretty funny, Leo. C'mon, let's go for a ramble around the local park'.

SCENE FROM A SURGERY—PADDY AND SARAH ARE A COUPLE VISITING THEIR DENTIST WHEN THE ASSISTANT ASKS PADDY TO FILL OUT A FORM.

PADDY: 'This form is a fairly tedious procedure, they are asking all kinds of questions about me. They want to know so much about my medical history, Sarah?'

SARAH: 'It's the first time you've been here, Paddy. The surgery probably want to get a brief idea of your background so they know it's safe to go ahead with the dentistry work'.

PADDY: 'Sweet Jesus. They must think I'm thick. Look here, beside where it asks for my name they have 'John Doe' as an example. Surely there can't be people who don't know their own name, ey?'

SARAH: 'They obviously have experience with some who are illiterate and don't understand certain things because they have issues. Don't be so dismissive of the form and just fill it in, will you?'

PADDY: 'John Doe and his sister Jane, ey?'!

SARAH: 'Yeah, that's true. At least you're lightening up darling'.

PADDY: 'And what about their relative from Liverpool who goes by the name 'Ah Buh Dee Doo Doe Don't Dee'?'!

THE TWO OF THEM CRACK UP.

SCENE FROM A CAR—A COUPLE, TOM AND JULIE, ARE DRIVING OUT OF THE CITY FOR A WEEKEND BREAK DOWN THE COUNTRY.

TOM: 'The traffic is fairly heavy with everybody heading out of Dublin for the long weekend, ey?'

JULIE: 'Yeah, it is Tom. Be careful not to get too frustrated, you know the statistics for road deaths at this time of the year'.

TOM: 'I'll try not to lose the rag too often darling'.

THEY EXIT THE CITY AND ARE IN THE PROVERBIAL ARSEH*LE.

JULIE: 'Tom, for feck sake be alert. A car could come out of nowhere down here. The locals are used to the roads being empty'.

TOM: 'Give it a rest, Julie. I know what I'm doing. See, it says on that sign post 'Dunmanway Next Left''.

JULIE: 'I know what it says ya know all. I saw the sign'.

TOM: 'Who do you think you are, a car passenger or the lead singer with Ace Of Base?'!

JULIE LIGHTENS UP.

JULIE: 'Fecking smart ass'!

TOM GIGGLES AWAY TO HIMSELF.

SCENE FROM A BUS—JONATHAN AND ALAN ARE ON A JOURNEY OUT OF THE CITY CENTRE TO THE SUBURBS OF DUBLIN AFTER THEIR DAY'S WORK.

JONATHAN: 'Are you going to watch the Merseyside derby on the box tonight, Al?'

ALAN: 'Yeah, I probably will. I hope the Reds pick up the three points we need'.

JONATHAN: 'So do I. It's a bit of a six-pointer with the Blues going for the European spots along with us'.

ALAN: 'I don't like the idea of us trying to bring that South African guy Innocent Mbwetemawayah in during the next transfer window. I think he just wants to join us for the money'.

JONATHAN: 'Let me tell ya, when Scousers proudly proclaim 'Passion, passion. Infinitely non-apart. Scouse brethren we are as one' they try to join the whole city of Liverpool regardless of what football side they favour and the last thing it is for is money, it's bourne out of love'!

ALAN: 'Yeah. I'm telling ya if those steel sculptures on top of The Liver Building were to fly over the ground on match day and sh*te, our fans couldn't see more of a fecking dirt-bird than that Mbwetemawayah fella'!

JONATHAN: 'Indeed. I hope we don't sign him either. I don't know who he thinks he's fooling with a name like Innocent. He's about as innocent as an incompetent banker mugging an old age pensioner in a charity shop on Budget Day, ey?'!

SCENE FROM A STREET—JER AND KEV ARE STROLLING DOWN TO THEIR LOCAL CHINESE TAKE-AWAY.

JER: 'Did you go for a pint last night, Kev?'

KEV: 'Yeah, didn't stay long though'.

JER: 'Why was that?'

KEV: 'I have to work this weekend and didn't want to be too tired getting up'.

JER: 'What time do you have to be up at when you work weekends?'

KEV: '5:45 a.m.'

JER: 'Good Lord. You should consider doing a milk delivery to bird nests on your way to the factory that's so early. You'd make a fortune'!

KEV: 'Yeah, that's an option to make extra income alright, Jer'!

THE MEN CHUCKLE AND MOVE ON TO CHAT ABOUT WHAT FOOD THEY MIGHT BUY WHEN THEY ARRIVE AT THE CHINESE.

SCENE FROM A FOOTBALL GROUND ON MERSEYSIDE—A TOPLESS FEMALE STREAKER HAS RUN ON TO THE PITCH.

ICKY: 'Ey Macca, look oveh theh la?' (Ey Macca, look over there la?)

MACCA: 'Wheh maytih?' (Where mate?).

ICKY: 'Theh. A toplish berd idge on the pitch'! (There. A topless bird is on the pitch!).

MACCA: 'Itch friggin' Janyoowerry, she musht be freedgin''! (It's friggin' January, she must be freezin'!).

ICKY: "old on a sheckind, datch Pamela Tittiefun darriz. Sheedge a pawn stah she idge'! (Hold on a second, that's Pamela Tittiefun that is. She's a porn star she is!).

MACCA: 'She came from dee away suppawttuz end'! (She came from the away supporters end!).

ICKY: 'An' ir wodge me thinkin' yoo'd ownlee fynd a peh of bloo titch at the berd owsh in yeh bahckk gahdin'! (And here was me thinkin' you'd only find a pair of blue tits at the bird house in your back garden!).

MACCA: 'H'har har. I thawht I'd ownlee eveh shee melon dropsdge in me lohkkill newdgeayhgintz'! (I thought I'd only ever see melon drops in my local newsagents'!

ICKY: 'Itch so cold I dohne know whetheh dowdge bloo melon titch ah goin' tih bownsh aw crahckk'! (It's so cold I don't know whether those blue melon tits are going to bounce or crack)!

MACCA: 'Go 'ead PALM-A-LOT Tittiefun'! (Go ahead PALM-
A-LOT Tittiefun!).

**THE PEOPLE AROUND THE TWO LADS HEAR THEM AND START
BELLOWING.**

SCENE FROM A SUMMER FAIR—A PENALTY SHOOT-OUT IS ABOUT TO TAKE PLACE AND A COUPLE OF TWINS ARE ENROLLING FOR IT WITH THE ORGANISER (TONY).

TONY: 'Hi fellas. You're obviously identical twins, aren't you?'

TWINS: 'We are, Mr. Walsh'.

TONY: 'What's your name?'

FIRST TWIN: 'Owen Lee'.

TONY WRITES HIS NAME ON THE SHEET AND THE TURNS TO THE OTHER TWIN.

TONY: 'And what's your name kiddo?'

SECOND TWIN: 'DeLoan'.

TONY IS WRITING HIS NAME DOWN WHEN SOMETHING SPARKS IN HIS SUB-CONSCIOUS.

TONY: 'Hold on a minute. Owen Lee. DeLoan Lee. Why do I think there's something familiar-sounding about that?'

OWEN: 'Our parents are big fans of Roy Orbison, Mr. Walsh'!

TONY: 'The two of you are messing me about, right?'!

DeLOAN: 'No, seriously Mr. Walsh. That's what our real names are'.

TONY: 'Your mam and dad have a warped sense of humour'!

OWEN: 'We are always being teased or people just think we are playing mind games'.

TONY: 'No probs. Go on and get prepared lads'!

SCENE FROM A BAR—A GROUP OF MEN ARE HAVING A FEW BEVERAGES.

MO: 'That Danny O'Callaghan is a very attractive-looking man, ey?'

BOYLER: 'Are you harbouring homo-sexual tendencies, Mo?'

MO: 'Feck off, Boyler. I'm a uni-cyclist'.

GAR: 'What does that mean?'

MO: 'It means I am hetero-sexual'.

GAR: 'So, does that mean a bi-cyclist is bi-sexual then?'

MO: 'Yeah, that's right'.

DONAL: 'What would you say about a tri-cyclist then? Not much I'd imagine'!

MICK: 'I know a bloke who could be described as being a tri-cyclist alright'!

MO: 'How in God's Name could someone be a tri-cyclist when there's only two genders?'

MICK: 'Well, not only does this bloke ride both men and women but because he picks his nose and scratches his ass in public, he's obviously 'f*cking gross' too, right?'!

THE GROUP OF GUYS LET A ROAR OF LAUGHTER OUT OF THEM.

SCENE FROM A PARTY—A COUPLE OF YOUNG LADS ARE HAVING SOME CRAIC SLAGGING ONE ANOTHER OFF AND BEING OVERLY COMPETITIVE.

ULLA: 'Hey Bang Bang. I've a greater chance of picking up a sexy chic at this party than you'!

BANG BANG: 'Why do you say that buddy?'

ULLA: 'Because I'm much better looking than you that's why'!

BANG BANG: 'Would you ever give it a fecking rest mate.'

ULLA: 'Shabba, shabba. We'll see how the night unfolds'!

BANG BANG: 'You're beginning to get me irritated. We're going to have to have a slight wager on this one'!

ULLA: 'Okay then. Fifty blips says I'll pick up a cracker before you'!

BANG BANG: 'You're on. I'm so irresistible even if I was a sportsman who got into politics and established the materialistic secular world order from a lap-dancing club, a staunch feminist would write 'Feck The Suffragettes' in lipstick across her bare breasts after getting a boob job done for me in a bookies in order to get me into the scratcher'!

ULLA: 'That's gas, Bang Bang. Bets are off. I wouldn't have the heart to take any money off you after coming out with something as good as that'!

SCENE FROM A SITTING ROOM—A COUPLE (SIOBHAN AND FIACRE) ARE CUDDLED UP ON THE COUCH WATCHING A MUSIC CHANNEL WHICH HAS A NIGHT DEDICATED TO LOVERS.

SIOBHAN: 'Oh, this is divine, Fiacre. Just you, me, a bottle of wine, an open fire and love songs'.

FIACRE: 'Yeah, I'm having a lovely time too darling'.

SIOBHAN: 'They're playing all our tunes too'.

FIACRE: 'You really are romantic, Siobhan. You're a pet, dote and exuder of angelic-ness'.

SIOBHAN: 'Thank you so much for saying that, Fiacre. I love you'.

FIACRE: 'I love you too'.

THE COUPLE GIVE EACH OTHER A KISS.

SIOBHAN: 'This is a great song'.

FIACRE: 'I don't recognise it. What's the title?'

SIOBHAN: ''I Swear (I Need You More Than Food)' by The Role Players'.

FIACRE: 'Oh, yeah. I remember it now. Do you know some Moroccan outfit covered this track?'

SIOBHAN: 'Are you serious?'

FIACRE: 'Yeah. But instead of calling the tune 'I Swear (I Need You More Than Food)' it was re-named as 'Cuss Cous'!

SIOBHAN CRACKS UP AND DOUBLES OVER WITH LAUGHTER.

SIOBHAN: 'You're so funny, Fiacre'!

FIACRE: 'Cheers, Siobh'.

THE COUPLE CONTINUE TO HUG EACH OTHER.

SCENE FROM A KITCHEN—TERRY HAS CALLED BY TO SEE HIS MATE (PAUL).

TERRY: 'Have you heard if Stef completed his cycle around the island of Ireland'?

PAUL: 'Funny you should mention it. I met him in town at the weekend and he said he got back to Dublin just last Tuesday'.

TERRY: 'What did he have to say about his exploits?'

PAUL: 'He said it was an amazing experience but that he was exhausted'.

TERRY: 'Exhausted, ey? Hadn't he been in training for over ten months before his trek?'

PAUL: 'He had mate. To be honest I'm certain 'train'ing is right as I'd say Iarnrod Eireann (the Irish rail network) took him along the majority of his journey'!

TERRY: 'Yeah. I'd say you're right knowing that fecker'!

PAUL: 'I promised him a night out on me if he did cycle all the way but I'll buy him just a pint now. That's about it'.

TERRY: 'Me too but I'll be interrogating him to get the truth about whether he actually did complete the journey on his bicycle before I do buy him that drink also'.

SCENE FROM A FOOTBALL MANAGER'S OFFICE—PADDY AND JIMMY ARE MAKING PLANS FOR AN OVER-65'S GAME.

PADDY: 'I tell ya, Jimmy. You really have to hand it to these old age pensioners. I mean, some of them are in the seventies and eighties and they are still as enthusiastic about the game as they've ever been judging by their attitude, ey?'

JIMMY: 'I know, Paddy. I hope I'm still alive at their age yet alone running around a football pitch'.

PADDY: 'They are at home this weekend, aren't they?'

JIMMY: 'They are. They're playing in the Freddie Zimmerman Memorial Trophy against a team from Ringsend?'

PADDY: 'What round is it?'

JIMMY: 'I think they are at the quarter-final stage. Hold on I'll check it out in the paper'.

JIMMY OPENS THE NEWSPAPER AND FLICKS THROUGH IT TO GET TO THE SPORTS SECTION.

JIMMY: 'There it is there, Paddy. They are actually playing in the semi-final stage of the Freddie . . . aw I don't believe it'!

JIMMY PASSES THE PAPER TO PADDY.

JIMMY: 'Take a look at what it says mate. I don't know whether to laugh or get furious'.

PADDY: 'For goodness sake. They have it mis-printed as the Freddie ZIMMERFRAME Memorial Trophy'!

JIMMY: 'Do you think it may be a bit of light-hearted fun?'

PADDY: 'I doubt it. Although maybe the editor does have a bit of a weird sense of humour'.

JIMMY: 'I'm sure the men will see the funny side of it, ey?'

PADDY: 'Hopefully they will'.

JIMMY SAYS HE IS GOING TO TEAR OUT THE PAGE, HIGHLIGHT THE ERROR AND PUT IT UP ON THE CLUB NOTICE BOARD FOR EVERYONE TO SEE. THE TWO GENTS HAVE A BIT OF A CHUCKLE.

SCENE FROM A BUTCHER'S SHOP—EDDIE AND HENRY ARE HAVING A CHAT.

EDDIE: 'Hey Henry. I recognised that person you've just served. I think he may be a neighbour of my uncle in Finglas. Do you know his name?'

HENRY: 'Do you mean that gentleman in the navy overcoat?'

EDDIE: 'Yeah mate'.

HENRY: 'Oh, that was Sonny Day. I used to get piano lessons off his daughter'.

EDDIE: 'Sonny Day? Are you taking the p*ss?'!

HENRY: 'I see where you are coming from but seriously that's his real name alright'.

EDDIE: 'Sonny Day and his Christian relatives Christmas and Easter Sun, ey?'!

HENRY: 'H'har har. Apparently his brother Patrick was a real 'saint'!

EDDIE: 'Or what about his father Zip A Dee Doo Dah Zip A Dee who was a bit of a 'character' back in the Forties'!

HENRY: 'Aw, stop it. I'll have pains in my sides if I laugh any more'!

SCENE FROM A STREET—BLAISE HAS BUMPED INTO HIS NEIGHBOUR (ANDY).

BLAISE:	'Alright Andy. What's the craic with you mate?'
ANDY:	'Grand thanks, Blaise. How about you?'
BLAISE:	'Yeah, I'm great too. I see Richie McConville has moved back in with Celine Hardy in number eleven'.
ANDY:	'That's right. They split up a few months back but they're back together a few weeks now'.
BLAISE:	'How long did they go out with each other for before they broke up?'
ANDY:	'It must have been for at least a decade'.
BLAISE:	'Apparently the fact that he lost his job as a wood machinist over in Harmonstown was a huge factor as he couldn't support Celine and her kids any more'.
ANDY:	'I'd say he must have got a new job elsewhere so, ey?'
BLAISE:	'Funny you should say that. I saw him being picked up by a van the other morning at about seven a.m. so he was probably on the way to work'.
ANDY:	'He was heading out for work alright. I'm telling you, he's only back living there because he's able to hand over three hundred euro a week to her'.
BLAISE:	'Of course he's giving her a few bob. He's not getting his log in for nothing'!

ANDY: 'H'har har. Trust you to think along those lines you dirty fecker. Having said that you're bang on. You get nothing for free these days, ey?'!

BLAISE: 'That's very true. Talk to you later pal'.

ANDY: 'See ya again soon buddy'.

SCENE FROM A DOCTOR'S SURGERY—JEM HAS BUMPED INTO HIS OLD PAL FITZ.

JEM: 'Hi there, Fitz. How are things mate? I haven't seen you around in a while'.

FITZ: 'Alright Jem. I'm fine thanks. I've been off the drink for the last six months. I wanted to get my weight down'.

JEM: 'Is that what you're here for then?'

FITZ: 'Yeah. I've an appointment with my GP to see if my blood pressure has come down. What has you here?'

JEM: 'Oh, I think I may have picked up a sexually transmitted disease. I got a ride off that Jennifer Malone at the weekend and I'm worried I have contracted something'.

FITZ: 'Jennifer Malone? I heard she wants sex like a b*stard'!

JEM: 'I know. I had a few gargles on me and couldn't resist the temptation'.

FITZ: 'She should be called Ho Malone she's so randy'!

JEM: 'Ho Malone? Why was she left behind by her family who were off on holiday around Christmas time as a child or something?'

FITZ: 'Oh, right. Ho Malone. I get it. Well it's not quite the festive season yet but if she has put me out of riding action over Yuletide, I'll be calling her Ho Ho Ho Malone'!

JEM: 'Ho Ho Ho Malone, ey? I like it mate'!

FITZ: 'Look, here comes Dr. O'Farrell. He's your doctor, isn't he? Go on, I'll talk to you later'.

JEM: 'I'll give you a bell at the weekend to see if you're up for a pint. Good luck'.

SCENE FROM A HOUSE—TOM HAS RECEIVED A CALL FROM HIS MATE (COSH) TO CATCH UP.

COSH: 'Hi Tom. It's Cosh here. What's the craic with you?'

TOM: 'Hi Cosh. I'm not too bad thanks. I'm just back from the shops'.

COSH: 'Are you about to have your dinner mate? I hope I'm not disturbing you'.

TOM: 'No, not yet. I wanted to cook something for myself but the butcher's wasn't open. Maybe there was a family bereavement or something'.

COSH: 'Have you not heard the news?'

TOM: 'What news?'

COSH: 'The place has closed down. Apparently Mr. O'Neill was fed up as he was making very little profit so he's cutting his losses. I was told he is considering opening a flower shop in Malahide'.

TOM: 'Ah, that's sad. I'll miss seeing him around. He was a nice man. He must have run that outlet for twenty years or more'.

COSH: 'Yeah, he was there for a long time alright. The missus told me a Chinese take-away is going to replace it but it's going to be run by an Irish family do you believe?'

TOM: 'An Irish family?'

COSH: 'That's right. Sam Cully and his brothers'.

TOM: 'The Cully's from the Drive?'

COSH: 'That's them'.

TOM: 'Hold on. You're pulling the p*ss, aren't you?'

COSH: 'No, I'm serious. Why? What do you mean?'

TOM: 'Well, just think about it. Sam Cully and his son who'll take the orders for the deliveries for the food called House Special Thai Plawn Gleen, right?'!

COSH: 'Oh, I see where you are coming from. H'ha har har, that's true. I never thought of the link. Wait 'til I tell Bertie. He'll find that funny'!

TOM: 'Yeah. Make sure to let him know that one alright. He'll get a good chuckle for sure'!

SCENE FROM A STREET—BUCKO HAS BUMPED INTO HIS PAL (GAGA) AND THEY ARE TALKING ABOUT THE RECESSION.

BUCKO: 'Story Gaga. What's the craic with ya? Have you managed to find another job yet?'

GAGA: 'Alright Bucko. No, I'm still on the scratcher but it's not for the lack of trying. I'm applying everywhere. No luck as yet though.'

BUCKO: 'Your wife must be browned off with always having you around the house, ey?'

GAGA: 'I suppose she is. When I'm not driving her to the supermarket, I'm driving her to distraction'!

BUCKO: 'That's one way of looking at it'!

GAGA: 'Ah, no. She's a pillar of strength in fairness and understands I'm doing my best'.

BUCKO: 'It's good to hear that mate'.

GAGA: 'Materialistic usurpers cause so much inequality and tribulation, don't they?'

BUCKO: 'I know. Elitists schmelitists'!

GAGA: 'True. I'll just have to keep saying my prayers for a breakthrough but the kids are a joy'.

BUCKO: 'Those greedy people, some try to cheat us. Blessed be the orchard-ness of a woman's womb, Foetus'!

GAGA: 'Very funny, Bucko. I can't say I've heard that one before'.

BUCKO: 'Keep applying for stuff and keep the sunny side out if you can pal. I'll keep you in my prayers. Best of luck. Talk to ya soon'.

GAGA: 'Cheers Bucko. I'll be in touch if I get anything'.

SCENE FROM A SITTING ROOM—GIT HAS ARRIVED HOME FROM HAVING BEEN IN THE BOOZER FOR A FEW HOURS. HIS WIFE (MARIA) AND SON (WILLIAM) ARE WATCHING THE NEWS.

GIT: 'Alreet Maria. Giz a kiss der love'. (Alright Maria. Give me a kiss there love).

MARIA: 'No, I won't, Git. You're drunk'.

GIT: 'No probs. Turn on de golf, William'.

WILLIAM: 'Hey mam. Tell dad I'd like to watch the end of the news'.

MARIA: 'He wants to watch the rest of the news, Git. It'll be finished in a few minutes. He likes to know the weather in particular. You can watch the golf then'.

GIT: 'Sound'.

CUT TO A SCENE FIVE MINUTES LATER. THE NEWS IS OVER AND WILLIAM RE-TUNES THE BOX AND THE GOLF COMES ON.

MARIA: 'Would you like a cup of tea, Git?'

GIT: 'Cheers Merree-eh. Darrid be grayh'. (Cheers Maria. That would be great).

MARIA LEAVES THE ROOM TO GO TO THE KITCHEN AND PUT THE KETTLE ON.

GIT: 'What's diss son? I don't reckignyiz dah golfaw, ee has veree long hayaw'. (What's this son? I don't recognise that golfer, he has very long hair).

WILLIAM: 'It's women's golf dad'.

GIT: 'Ah, datz a load of me b*llix. I was hoping to see dah Spanish fella Sergio Miguel Jimenabalezcia'!

WILLIAM: 'Some of these women are very good dad. They are all scratch golfers'.

GIT: 'Oyim owenlee intawrestid in how de game iz playid naw if dee have feminine itch also'! (I'm only interested in how the game is played not if they have feminine itch also!).

WILLIAM STARTS GIGGLING.

GIT: 'Datz my boy'! (That's my boy!).

WILLIAM: 'Hey dad. You're picking away at your hoop so does that mean you're a scratch basketball player'!

GIT: 'Come heeaw, William. Yiv gaw my sense of humaw. Love ya pal'. (Come here, William. You've got my sense of humour. Love ya pal).

WILLIAM GOES OVER TO HIS DAD AND THEY HUG EACH OTHER.

SCENE FROM AN OFFICE—DAVID AND SIMON ARE HAVING A CHAT ABOUT WORK. THEY ARE EMPLOYED BY AN ASSET MANAGEMENT COMPANY.

DAVID: 'I think I'm going to be in trouble, Simon'.

SIMON: 'Why do you say that?'

DAVID: 'I've left the portfolio manager out of the e-mail with a major pre-advice once again. That's the second time this week I've messed up in that respect'.

SIMON: 'You did the pricing on a fund you shouldn't have just a few days ago too, didn't you?'

DAVID: 'Yeah, that's right. I think the dealing manager will be having words with me before long. These kind of mistakes are easily avoided, ey?'

SIMON: 'Don't be too stressed. You are not in the department long. Do you know Steve in cash management?'

DAVID: 'I do. I met him in the canteen yesterday'.

SIMON: 'Well, he takes days off which his boss Amanda knows are not genuine sick days. He was also caught having a liquid lunch last month. He's always in the dog house but gets away with it all the time. Don't fret, your manager will understand you're 'dealing' with a lot of new stuff. Pardon the pun'!

DAVID: 'Cheers for re-assuring me, Simon. Maybe I haven't done anything too punishable'.

SIMON: 'Exactly. If the Birdman of Alcatraz was incarcerated
            on a dozen occasions, he couldn't get out of jail more
            often than Steve'!

DAVID: 'H'har har. That's very funny. I should lighten up and
            refrain from worrying too much for sure'.

SCENE FROM A PUB—A GROUP OF YOUNG LADS ARE OUT DRINKING A FEW PINTS AND ARE HAVING A GREAT TIME SLAGGING PEOPLE OFF.

SCRUFF: 'Would yiz look at the bleedin' state of that oul one coming back from the bar'!

JAHZER: 'That's Paulie Jeffries auntie Martina'.

BOMBER: 'She must be in her early sixties and she's wearing a skirt. Talk about mutton dressed as lamb'.

SCRUFF: 'Mutton Jeffries, ey? We won't have to keep our voices down as she probably wouldn't be able to hear us anyway'!

JAHZER: 'She should start her own hearing aids company and call it Mutton Jeffries alright. Although she looks well for an oul dear in fairness'!

BOMBER: 'You always have had a bit of a thing for the older woman, Jahzer. She's a married woman so forget about it mate'.

SCRUFF: 'Her husband works in the abattoire out in Skerries. He'll chop your mickey off if he finds out you were eyeing up his missus'!

JAHZER: 'Imagine how attractive she was twenty five years ago. I'd say he has slaughtered her on a few occasions alright'!

THE BLOKES START LAUGHING AND TRY TO FIND SOMEBODY ELSE TO POKE FUN AT.

SCENE FROM A HOUSE—PODGE IS ON THE PHONE TO HIS MATE DIXIE WHO'S A DWARF.

PODGE: 'What are you getting up to this evening, Dixie?'

DIXIE: 'Oh, after I have my dinner I'll probably watch the football on the box'.

PODGE: 'I suppose a box is what you need to step up on to get on to the couch anyway, ey?'!

DIXIE: 'Feck off mate'.

PODGE: 'Ah, sorry pal. I hope you have an entertaining night with the game. Enjoy yourself and put your feet up'!

DIXIE: 'Are you taking the p*ss again, Podge?'

PODGE: 'What do you mean?'

DIXIE: 'Well, when I sit on a couch there's only one place my feet can go and that is up'!

PODGE: 'I seen what you mean'.

DIXIE: 'And even when I stand up I'm still only half way up in comparison to most people too'!

PODGE: 'I get your point. You certainly didn't create the foot-rest and if you had it definitely wasn't for yourself, right?'!

DIXIE: 'Yeah, that's an interesting one buddy. Ha ha'!

PODGE: 'Good to see you're retaining your sense of humour. Talk to you soon'.

DIXIE: 'Take good care'.

SCENE FROM A STUDIO OFFICE—CORMAC IS VISITING HIS PAL, MICK, WHO HAS HIS OWN ADVERTISING BUSINESS.

CORMAC: 'Hey Mick. Great to see you buddy'.

MICK: 'Ah, Cormo. Haven't seen you in a while. How have you been?'

CORMAC: 'I've been struggling. I'm recovering from a psychotic episode. I have schizophrenia. Couldn't have been more stressed but I'm recovering all the time'.

MICK: 'Sorry to hear that. What doesn't kill you makes you stronger, ey?'

CORMAC: 'Maybe. But I remember encountering a totally beautiful female out in Tamangos before who didn't kill me but (because my head got light, my heart started thumping and my knees buckled) I became as weak as the butterflies in my stomach struggling to bench press helium'!

MICK: 'H'har har, Cormo. At least you are still able to crack a joke. Fair play to you'.

THE TWO GUYS EXIT THE STUDIO TO GET A COFFEE AND CONTINUE CATCHING UP.

SCENE FROM A GAELIC SPORTS GROUND—AN IMPORTANT CLUB GAME IS BEING PLAYED. THERE IS ONLY A SINGLE POINT IN THE DIFFERENCE AND THE TEAM WHO ARE CHASING THE MATCH ARE BREAKING UP-FIELD WITH ONLY SECONDS LEFT ON THE CLOCK. THE SLIOTHAR (THE BALL WHICH IS USED IN HURLING) IS HIT FROM FORTY METRES AND BISECTS THE UPRIGHTS BUT THE UMPIRE SIGNALS A WIDE. TWO YOUNG BOYS ARE STANDING BEHIND THE GOAL.

JOVIS:　　　'Can you believe that Bermac?'

BERMAC:　　'No I can't. That umpire is a fecking cheating so-and-so'.

AT THIS STAGE A RIOT IS BREAKING OUT WITH THE PLAYERS AND COACHING TEAM OF THE SIDE THAT HAVE BEEN DENIED THE LEVELLING SCORE CONFRONTING THE CROOKED UMPIRE. ALL SORTS OF ABUSE, OBSCENITIES AND INSULTS ARE BEING HURLED (PARDON THE PUN!).

JOVIS:　　　'I don't blame them for getting angry. That was definitely a score, ey?'

BERMAC:　　'Of course it was. It's perfectly obvious that bloke doesn't want extra-time. The various sorting offices of the entire world's mail couldn't split their respective 'posts' any better than what that half-forward has just done'!

JOVIS:　　　'There's bleedin' war breaking out. Look at the face on their head coach. He's like a sunburnt, whiskey-drinking beetroot he's so angry'!

BERMAC:　　'C'mon Jovis. Let's get out of here before we get caught up in this madness'.

SCENE FROM A CRICKET CLUBHOUSE—A COUPLE OF A SIDE'S MANAGEMENT TEAM ARE HAVING A DISCUSSION ABOUT THEIR SELECTION POLICY.

NICK: 'We've gone through the batting order now it's time to select a captain, Trevor'.

TREVOR: 'Reese Chisholm would be my choice as he seems to have a good tactical brain and leadership qualities'.

NICK: 'Yeah. I agree with you to a point but do you think he has the capabilities to see the bigger picture at an important point of a close Twenty20 intercounty match?'

TREVOR: 'Mmm. That's food for thought. He did captain his school to the championship a few years back so I reckon he'd do alright'.

NICK: 'It's my opinion he might need more imagination out in the field as he doesn't seem to be spatially inclined'.

TREVOR: 'Well, I'm sure he'd have more imagination out in the field than a bicycle-spoke-collecting Belgian scarecrow who dresses himself in nothing but mid-grey all the time anyway'!

NICK: 'I'm sure he'd have more imagination than that for sure! Let's go with him, Trev. We've nothing to lose'.

SCENE FROM A LIVING ROOM—RICHIE HAS POPPED AROUND TO SEE HIS PAL (MO).

RICHIE: 'How's your new book coming along, Mo?'

MO: 'Oh, not too bad thanks. I thought I had it completed earlier this week but I edited out the concluding chapter as it was not up to scratch'.

RICHIE: 'Fair play to you for getting it written so quickly. By the way, where's Sophie (Mo's wife)?'

MO: 'Cheers mate. Sophie is not getting out of bed because she's afraid she'll pass on the scabies she's contracted to one of us'.

RICHIE: 'Oh, I see. So she's 'not up to scratch' either, ey?'!

MO: 'Very good, Richie. I suppose it would be safe to say she's staying in the scratcher for sure, right?'!

RICHIE: 'All we need is for you to lose your job, go on the dole yourself and there'll be even more scratching done by the occupants of this household than when a group of blind thirty six handicappers play a professional links course in windy conditions'!

MO: 'Funny man, Richie. Funny man'.

SCENE FROM A CAR—GEORGE AND CELINE ARE DRIVING HOME HAVING DONE A BIT OF SHOPPING. THE RADIO IS ON.

GEORGE: 'Is that the news coming on now, Celine?'

CELINE: 'It is. Would you like me to turn up the volume slightly?'

GEORGE: 'Yeah. Please do'.

VOICE FROM THE RADIO: 'A super typhoon has hit south east Asia bringing winds in excess of two hundred and seventy five kilometres per hour along with it and causing much devastation in the region'.

GEORGE: 'That's terrible, isn't it? I hope the people can find shelter for themselves'.

CELINE: 'I know. Let's pray they'll be okay. We're lucky we don't get those extremes here in Ireland'.

GEORGE: 'A 'super' typhoon, ey? Well I tell ya I'd hate to see the destruction an OUT-AND-OUT ABSOLUTE B*STARD typhoon would cause'!

CELINE GIGGLES BUT COMMENTS TO GEORGE THAT THIS ISN'T THE TIME TO BE CRACKING JOKES DURING A SENSITIVE PERIOD FOR FELLOW HUMAN BEINGS. GEORGE AGREES AND PROMISES HE WILL MAKE A SMALL DONATION TO A CHARITY THAT DEALS WITH HELPING PEOPLE AFFECTED BY NATURAL DISASTERS DURING THE UP-COMING WEEK.

SCENE FROM A HEALTH CENTRE—BARRY IS WAITING TO SEE A SPECIALIST AND GETS TALKING TO ANOTHER PATIENT (STEPHEN).

BARRY: 'Alright mate. What has you here?'

STEPHEN: 'Oh, I'm having some problems with my mental welfare. How about you?'

BARRY: 'I'm suffering from schizophrenia. I've been recovering for the last decade but been stable for about five years now'.

STEPHEN: 'What's the name of the organisation attached to people with mental ill health here called'.

BARRY: 'Shine'.

STEPHEN: 'Shine, ey? I thought it went by another name'.

BARRY: 'It was called Schizophrenia Ireland up until a few years back'.

STEPHEN: 'I suppose they probably changed the name because schizophrenia isn't the only kind of mental illness, ey?'

BARRY: 'Yeah, that's true. However there could have been establishments in other countries entitled 'Depression Russia', 'Alzheimer's Algeria' or how about 'Dementia Democratic Republic of Congo"!

STEPHEN: 'Ha ha. You could even have 'Bi-Polar Arctic-Antartic' if you think about it, ey?!

BARRY: 'Ha ha. It's good that we can have a bit of a laugh about our difficulties, right?'

STEPHEN: 'Indeed. No point in taking yourself too seriously although maybe it's not the best thing to be joking about. Some might deem it cruel'.

BARRY: 'I suppose that's true to a point but it's still uplifting to poke some fun with someone who is able to enjoy a giggle'.

THE TWO GUYS MOVE ON TO TALKING ABOUT DIFFERENT TOPICS BEFORE THEIR PSYCHIATRISTS ARRIVE.

SCENE FROM AN INTERNET FORUM—A WAR OF WORDS HAS BROKEN OUT BETWEEN A COUPLE OF FOOTBALL FANS.

SCOUSER: 'Six Times European Champions mate. Six Times European Champions'!

MANC: 'What the feck are you on about ya Scouse b*stard. That's pure fantasy. You've only won it five times'.

SCOUSER: 'I'm tellin' ya matey, Six Times European Champions'!

MANC: 'Shut up. How about Twenty Times, Twenty Times'!

SCOUSER: 'Twenty times, ey? That's the amount of occasions you had a tug on your birthday before you were old enough to get an alcoholic beverage served to you in New York'!

MANC: 'FIVE TIMES. You Scousers are ones to be talking about tugging, you show off your beasts with FIVE fingers to us all the time'!

SCOUSER: 'Six Times European Champions'!

MANC: 'Dream on, Scouser. It's only five times'.

SCOUSER: 'I'm a Scouse prophet. Six Times European Champions'!

MANC: 'Feck off ya Scouse b*stard'!

SCOUSER: 'I'm a Scouse prophet. Shixxx Times Yehropean Champeeinge. SHIXXX TIMES YEHROPEAN CHAMPEEINGE'!

MANC: 'We'll see buddy. All you Scouse football fans are scum anyway'.

SCOUSER: 'You Mancs calling us Scousers 'scum' is like Neanderthal men calling baboons 'the hairy arseh*les' given the amount of abuse you dish out our way'!

THE INTERACTION CONTINUES . . . .

SCENE FROM A BEDROOM—A COUPLE OF YOUNG FRIENDS (ROSS AND SEAN) ARE LISTENING TO THE RADIO.

ROSS: 'Let's play a game of 'Beat the Intro', Sean'.

SEAN: 'Yeah. That'll be a bit of craic'.

A SONG COMES ON WHICH THE TWO OF THEM ARE HAVING DIFFICULTY IN RECOGNISING.

ROSS: 'Aw, I think it's on the tip of my tongue'.

SEAN: 'It's coming to me too'.

ROSS: 'I'm certain the title is 'Breaking My Heart All Over Again' but I'm struggling with the artist'.

SEAN: 'Oh, they're called 'Neanderthal Men In Drag' or something.

ROSS GOES INTO A FIT.

ROSS: 'I've figured it out. You're along the right lines mate. The band are called 'Queens of the Pre-historic Age'!

BOTH BOYS FALL ABOUT THE ROOM LAUGHING.

SCENE FROM AN OFFICE—KEITH IS A CIVIL SERVANT AND IS TALKING TO HIS BOSS (GAVIN).

KEITH: 'Okay Gavin, you're probably wondering why I have asked to speak to you here in the boardroom, are you?'

GAVIN: 'Well I have to say I am, Keith. Is everything alright?'

KEITH: 'I've been working in this department for over fifteen years and I think I need a bit of a change'.

GAVIN: 'You're not thinking of leaving the Civil Service altogether, are you?'

KEITH: 'No, but I would like to change to a different area if possible'.

GAVIN: 'Have you anything particular in mind?'

KEITH: 'I don't really know. I'd like a freer role though. Could you suggest something maybe?'

GAVIN: 'You seem to have a passion for justice. Would you consider police vetting?'

KEITH: 'Feck off, Gavin. If you think I'm interested in checking out an Alsatian's teeth and seeing if it has worms in its' coat while it's fighting off football hooligans, forget about it mate'!

GAVIN: 'Very good, Keith. But seriously they do great work in protecting vulnerable people. I'd say you'd enjoy that sort of thing'.

KEITH: 'Yeah, thanks Gav. I'll give it some thought over the next while'.

GAVIN: 'Good man. I'm sure you'll make the right decision eventually. Let me know when you're going to make the move'.

KEITH: 'Cheers'.

SCENE FROM AN INDIAN TAKE-AWAY IN THE U.K—DECO IS ON A STAG WEEKEND FROM DUBLIN AND ENTERS THE ESTABLISHMENT DECIDING HE WANTS TO HAVE A BIT OF FUN WITH THE STAFF.

DECO: 'Alright bud. What's the craic with ya?'

ASSISTANT: 'Oh, I do be doing very well thank you'.

DECO: 'Are you from India mate?'

ASSISTANT: 'I am'.

DECO: 'What part?'

ASSISTANT: 'I am from Mumbai'.

DECO: 'Did your 'mum buy' you that very colourful top you're wearing?! Well, tell her from me it's really loud! What's your name?'

ASSISTANT: 'My name is Raj Singh'.

DECO: 'Doesn't sound like you're singing to me but talking ya bleedin' raja'!

ASSISTANT: 'I do be thinking you are being a bit rude. Do you want to be ordering food, sir?'

DECO: 'I don't recognise anything on the menu. I haven't tried any of these dishes before. Could you suggest some sort of a mild curry with lamb?'

ASSISTANT: 'How about number twenty three?'

DECO: 'Yeah, that looks nice. How do you pronounce the name of it?'

ASSISTANT: 'Lobia Gosht'.

DECO: 'Yeah, I'll have the 'Front-bum Phantom' with pilau rice please'!

ASSISTANT: 'You are being very bold, sir. That will be £6.95 please'.

DECO: 'Cheers'.

ASSISTANT: 'It will be with you in about ten minutes, sir. Please take a seat'.

SCENE FROM A DRIVE-WAY—TONY AND NOEL HAVE DECIDED TO WASH TONY'S WIFE'S (JENNA) CAR.

TONY: 'This motor is in a bit of a state, ey?'

NOEL: 'It is. Jenna must have been driving along country roads during a rainy period or something. Look at all the mud splashed up the sides'.

TONY: 'It'll take us a while to get it spick and span. I think we'll power hose it then give it a waxing, ey?'

NOEL: 'Yeah, that's a good idea'.

TONY: 'Goodness me, there's a load of bird sh*t on the windscreen too'.

NOEL: 'A load is right. She must have been parked under a tree'.

TONY: 'I reckon it's more likely the car was under a bird's ass myself'!

NOEL: 'Ha ha. That's very true. C'mon, let's get stuck into this job'.

BOTH MEN WALK OFF TO THE GARAGE LAUGHING.

SCENE FROM A HOUSE—PLUG HAS CALLED INTO SEE HIS BROTHER (SPARKS).

PLUG: 'Alright Sparks. How have you been keeping bro?'

SPARKS: 'Ah, I'm grand thanks. You haven't been in touch in a while'.

PLUG: 'I just moved house recently so I've been up to my eyes with getting everything and everyone settled in my new place'.

SPARKS: 'Is that so? Where are you living now?'

PLUG: 'Edenmore'.

SPARKS: 'Oh, I see. The locals called that place The 'More'.

PLUG: 'Do they?'

SPARKS: 'Yeah, but because most have strong Dublin accents, they pronounce it as De 'Moer'.

PLUG: 'Well, I can relate to the whole De 'Moer thing alright because up until the end of the Summer young fellas were calling at my front door every ten minutes asking did I want to have the grass cut'!

BOTH MEN CRACK UP.

SCENE FROM A DEPARTMENT STORE IN DUBLIN'S CITY CENTRE - JAY AND OLIVE ARE OUT SHOPPING IN THE RUN UP TO CHRISTMAS.

JAY: 'There's so much to choose from, Olive. I don't know where to be looking'.

OLIVE: 'Well, just think about what you will be needing for the festive period'.

JAY: 'I've to get my boss in work a kris kindle present. I drew him out of the hat during the week'.

OLIVE: 'What's the most you can spend on the gift?'

JAY: 'Ten euro. Although I can't stand him. He's as tight-fisted. I don't like him and don't want to be getting anything for him at all'.

OLIVE: 'He's mean, ey?'

JAY: 'Yeah, he wouldn't give you the steam off his p*ss'.

OLIVE: 'Oh, I see. So you certainly won't be splashing out on an expensive after shave or anything for him, right?'

JAY: 'Mmm. It's Christmas I suppose so I might slash into a bottle and give him some of my own Cologne called 'Fine Is Urine', the new fragrance from Cavan Inclined! It would be a good way of getting my own back on the stingy so-and-so'!

OLIVE: 'That's gross, Jay. Maybe he'd deserve it though'.

JAY: 'He most certainly would. He never gave me that raise I asked for back in August. Remember?'

OLIVE: 'I do remember. Just buy him the first cheap thing you see. Don't go to the bother of putting too much thought into it'.

THE COUPLE CONTINUE TO BROWSE AROUND.

SCENE FROM A GOLF CLUB—A COUPLE (GARY AND SANDRA) ARE OUT HAVING A DRINK AND ARE WATCHING ALL OF THE PLAYERS COMING UP THE EIGHTEENTH.

GARY: 'Here comes Mickey Mast. He plays off scratch. I imagine he's burned up the course today as he knows it like the back of his hand and these conditions would really suit him'.

SANDRA: 'So, he's a good player, is he?'

GARY: 'Yeah, he is. He wins a lot of competitions. I don't think you'd like him though'.

SANDRA: 'Why do you say that?'

GARY: 'He's a bit of a chauvinist. He doesn't believe women should be allowed to become playing members and if he had his way, no females would be permitted to have a drink in this lounge'.

SANDRA: 'I don't like the sound of him one bit. Look at the state of him. Mickey Mast, ey? He's so unattractive if he had any respect for us ladies at all, he'd fly a sexually repressed country's flag out of it when he's excited'!

GARY: 'That's gas, San! Don't say that too loud again while you're in here though as if someone was to overhear that we could be barred'.

SANDRA: 'As if I could be bothered with being barred from a male chauvinist pig hang-out, Gary'.

GARY: 'I don't blame you. C'mon, give me your hand and we'll go for a walk while the sun is setting. That'll be a better way to end the day. Nice and romantic'.

SCENE FROM A RADIO STATION STUDIO—A TALK SHOW HOST HAS INVITED PEOPLE TO CALL IN AND TELL HIM WHY THEIR PARENTS DECIDED TO GIVE THEM THE NAME THEY HAVE.

DEEJAY: 'Okay then. Let's go to line four. Who have we got here?'

CALLER: 'Hi. My name is Holly'.

DEEJAY: 'I think I can see where this one is coming from. Were you born around Christmas time?'

HOLLY: 'Yeah, that's right'.

DEEJAY: 'That's lovely, Holly. Nice name. Thank you for your call. Take care. Let's go to line two. Hi, you're live on air. What's your name?'

CALLER: 'Hi. I'm called LeTraque'.

DEEJAY: 'Sounds like a French name. Am I right?'

LETRAQUE: 'You're correct. My mother is from Paris and she ran the ten thousand metres a lot when she was younger'!

DEEJAY: 'Is that so? I thought you were going to tell me your dad was a pretentious train driver or something! Very interesting. Cheers for your call, LeTraque. Okay, the final caller on this. Let's go to line five. Hello there. What did your parents Christen you?'

CALLER: 'Felectricity'.

DEEJAY: 'Sweet Jesus. Where on earth did your parents come up with a name like that?'

FELECTRICITY: 'My mother's name is Felicity and my dad insisted on the name because he got her up the pole while he was up the pole a lot himself as he used to work as a line-man for a major power company'!

THE DEEJAY CRACKS UP.

DEEJAY: 'I think I've heard it all now. Your parents should be arrested for being so cruel. Take care, Felectricity'!

SCENE FROM A SOCIAL NETWORKING SITE - SOME SOCCER FANS ARE MAKING COMMENTS ABOUT ONE OF THE DAY'S BIG GAMES.

WOBBLE: 'That was a good game today, ey?'

CORMO: 'It was but I'm fuming. The Reds were denied a definite penalty. It should have been given and had we scored it, might have got something out of the game'.

WOBBLE: 'I know. I'm frustrated too. For not giving us that decision, the ref needs to have his eyes tested'.

CORMO: 'Too right but he never gives us anything. Our fans always give him grief so he's probably afraid to give us the big decisions lest the opposition supporters get on his back as well'.

WOBBLE: 'Well I tell ya, Cormo if he's going to miss the blatant obvious like he did today, he's not going to get the higher profile matches on the continent and on the international scene also. I think he's useless to be honest'.

CORMO: 'He is. I can't stand him. He's about as useful as a gay thalidomide trying to give his lover (who's a baby-oil-drenched sumo wrestler) a 'reach around' with boxing gloves on during sex'!

WOBBLE: 'Bahahaha. That's deadly. I can't wait to tell the rest of the crew that one'!

CORMO: 'Yeah. Make sure to tell the lads that one but you better give me the credit for coming up with it'!

WOBBLE: 'Don't worry. They'll know that's exactly the sort of thing you'd come out with'!

CORMO: 'Cheers, Wobble. I might meet up with you all sometime over the St. Patrick's weekend'.

WOBBLE: 'Do that. We'd love to see you. It's been a while'.

SCENE FROM A STREET—TONY HAS BUMPED INTO HIS FRIEND (DAR DAR) AND HAS SOME GOSSIP.

TONY: 'Alright Dar Dar. What's the craic with ya mate?'

DAR DAR: 'Ah, not too bad thanks. Just feeling a bit tired after working a long shift'.

TONY: 'Wait and I'll tell ya what I heard today. I bumped into Buzz O'Connor earlier. He said he was talking to that bloke who lives on his own in the corner house and he told him that he's The Counsellor'.

DAR DAR: 'Do you mean he's The Holy Spirit?'

TONY: 'That's exactly what I mean. He said Jesus Christ alluded to him being The Light of the World during His Sermon on the Mount and that the town that is set in a hill which The Lord referred to is in relation to Sutton and Howth (on Dublin's north side). He continued that Christ immediately revealed 'nor do you take a Lamp out and put it under a bowl. Don't you put it on its' stand, it gives light to the whole house. So let your light shine before men so that they give praise to your Father in Heaven'.

DAR DAR: 'You're going to have to explain that to me, Tony'.

TONY: 'The Lamp is what signifies The Holy Spirit. He's asserting that Jesus is re-assuring him he should have nothing to fear by being famous. He is also maintaining that The Lord is telling him not to be afraid of being in the house on his own after the passing of his parents that's why He said 'it gives light to the whole house' because he suffers from schizophrenia and sometimes feels a little frightened at night. He says Jesus purposely used the word 'shine' as Shine is the organisation attached to people with mental ill health here in Ireland'!

DAR DAR: 'Woh. That's powerful stuff. But Jesus said 'so that they give praise to your Father in Heaven'. Does that not mean all of God's children, no?'

TONY: 'I asked him that too but he said that he is The Light of the World because he is here in the world on this planet and while he lives here he is part-animal and thus a son while he does reside on earth. He told me Jesus referred to Himself as The Light of the World too and nobody else can claim to be equal to The Lord but he can because all three parts in The Blessed Trinity are equi-powerful'!

DAR DAR: 'I don't know what to say to that but I'm not going to deny it's definitely all registering with me and making perfect sense as The Lamp would exude light for sure'.

TONY: 'Yeah, he said it will be snuffed out if you are wicked. I've more to tell ya. He also says he is going to be martyred on the streets of Jerusalem along with what he calls 'the other witness' who he says is the other Lamp as documented in the Book of Revelations'!

DAR DAR: 'What? Tell me more'.

TONY: 'He said this part of Scripture is written in the past tense and that he had a dream about his resurrection about seven years ago. He said in this dream he had a vision from what he believes is The Last Supper and he said Jesus was looking at Himself in a mirror. He asserts that this was Jesus advising him that is like the proverbial mirror himself. He told me the next thing he experienced was being covered in glory, could hear people crying and a lady called out his name. He says that he is going to be brought back to life in front of the whole world three and a half days later (as is also referred to in the Book of Revelations) and is going off to Heaven in a blaze of glory'!

DAR DAR: 'Are you serious? That's why he was able to have the dream. As you said this part of Scripture is written in the past tense so it has already happened in The Eyes of God, right?'

TONY: 'Yeah, that's true alright'.

DAR DAR: 'He's very quiet this bloke, isn't he?'

TONY: 'I decided to chat to him only a couple of hours ago and he says he doesn't drink, smoke, gamble, do drugs or eat pig meat. He also said he hates the materialistic order which has been established because it's what will enable the son of perdition to crush spirits some time in the near future. That's why he hates secular politics too and believes The Beast will be a politician. He said St. Malachy was shown a vision of the future and that it was revealed to him there would be 112 popes after a certain time, then the end will come. Have a guess what number Francis is?'!

DAR DAR: 'I don't know. How about 110th?'

TONY: 'No. Francis is the 112th. He told me he will probably be usurped by 'the false prophet' who will be the religious leader whom the son of perdition will turn to to be backed up as a way of trying to deceive the world that he is doing the right thing'!

DAR DAR: 'Goodness me'.

TONY: 'He also says he doesn't like games as it involves putting oneself under unnecessary pressure to achieve completely inanimate outcomes'!

DAR DAR: 'He's a bit religious this fella, ey?'

TONY: 'Well, that's just it. He believes Jesus and God dislike religion and that it is more about having an intimate relationship with The Almighty and His Son instead'!

DAR DAR: 'This bloke is a bit of a republican too, isn't he?'

TONY: 'I asked him that aswell but he says he would much prefer to be regarded as a peaceful Irish freedomist. He understands the British in Ulster's gripe with certain aspects of Roman Catholicism but thinks we should all live together in harmony as that what Jesus Christ would want us to do. He says that above all else the day of his resurrection will be a day for a united Ireland. He says he is going to put all of this in his next book'!

DAR DAR: 'It will get a lot of people talking. I think I might buy it. What's it going to be called?'

TONY: 'He doesn't know what he is going to entitle it yet but as a child-like laugh he's thinking of using the pseudonym 'Chuck E. R. Law''!

DAR DAR: 'That would be controversial but he's just having a bit of a harmless josh I suppose'.

TONY: 'Wait, I've even more to tell ya. He proposed something to me. He asked me did I believe in God and I said 'yes'. He then asked me did I believe one day His Holy Spirit would come to planet earth and I responded 'yes' again. He continued did I think one day the son of perdition would exist and I replied that I did. He went on that the son of perdition has been walking the face of planet earth and he has these delusions that he is God, he wants to be exalted and worshipped as God and earth is the only dominion in the universe where Lucifer can be exalted and worshipped as God. Then he is coming to the planet as genuine one-third-part in The GOD Head to scupper The Beast's plans to be exalted and worshipped as God and drag as many spirits into the 'lake of fire' as he can with him. He asked what I thought and I immediately deduced 'a conspiracy'. He said that it was his knowledge that this is the truth, that it was a no-brainer and I agreed'!

DAR DAR: 'What? Did he continue'.

TONY: 'He did. He said that he has been abused by evil media men ever since he was in his mother's womb, that they even knew at least some of his thoughts and they did everything they could to take him out of the equation. He continued that he is the force restraining 'the seed of Lucifer' as referred to in the Book of Thessalonians because he's the genius in his sub-conscious that he doesn't want to have to contend with and that's why they purposely positioned themselves to destroy his welfare. He asserts they de-proponentised him having any sort of quality of life'!

DAR DAR: 'That's what he said? Go on, tell me more'.

TONY: 'He continued that ever since he was a baby the evil media men had been immersing him regarding the actualities in his life, ridiculing him for every child-like mistake made and making him responsible for everything he did, said and even thought in many respects'!

DAR DAR: 'How did they know about everything that was going on with him?'

TONY: 'He insisted that he didn't want to share what he knows is the truth with me but just asked me to figure things out for myself instead. He asked me to put two and two together and come up with what I thought in my own mind. Are you sensing what I am?'!

DAR DAR: 'Are you serious? I know what I'm believing'.

TONY: 'He explained that Lucifer masquerades as an 'angel of light' but he is the light because that's what a Lamp exudes. He says Lucifer won't accept that he is subordinate to him and that he is insanely jealous of him. He told me that Lucifer is trying to construe that he is the light on the side of God and that God is the bad guy. He continued that he is the light on the side of God (because he is a Lamp) and that God is very much 100% the good guy'!

DAR DAR: 'Feck me. Did he say anything else about the media?'

TONY: 'Yeah. He also explained that it was all part of these evil media men's plans that he get all the attention he didn't want including that which he was totally undeserving of. He said they were putting up a front of being on his side but spent the whole time in the interim mentally, emotionally and sexually abusing him. He continued that they were intent on turning everybody against one another particularly putting a strain on the relationship between the genders and various classes within society. He's saying they were mis-representing him and mis-construing everything. He's also saying they were driving wedges between him and relationships with other people particularly women. He's asserting they were trying to turn him into a paranoid and deluded loner while simultaneously inviting negative attention in to his life by perversifying his character and circumstances'!

DAR DAR: 'This is unreal'.

TONY: 'I'm not joking. He's maintaining these evil media men had been inducing him into making mistakes and were humiliating him by letting everyone know about his transgressions over the airwaves but it wasn't his fault he was making mistakes as he suffers from schizophrenia and was an extremely abused, repressed prisoner in his very being having his life relentlessly trespassed upon, his privacy invaded and his very being violated. He's also saying these men were deriving sporting terminologies relative to the actualities in his life knowing that they were angering, antagonising, aggravating and frustrating him because they knew he dislikes most sport talk particularly with regard to games'!

DAR DAR: 'Has he being saying any of this to anybody else?'

TONY: 'He told me he has been letting some sections of the media know because they are aware of who it is he is and he feels a lot more confident because the evil media men have been taken out of their positions'!

DAR DAR: 'So he's a media-God of some sort, ey? Wow'.

TONY: 'I suppose you could say that alright. He says he has always been afraid to share what he knows is the truth because he's worried the 'Golden Fleece' will get involved, not believe him and send him to jail when it should be the evil media men who should be sent to 'He Is Risen"'!

DAR DAR: 'I don't know what to say to all of that, Tony. This guy has some imagination'.

TONY: 'He does. Neither do I. I'm telling ya the bloke will be diagnosed as either mad or a genius one day although he told me a professional advised him that he is a genius. He was also informed he has the mental age of a one year old due to regression'.

DAR DAR: 'Mmm. If he was advised he's a genius, we have to respect the professional's assessment, ey? He's just a baby aswell. He must never know what to make of anything. Pure and total innocence'.

TONY: 'I know. We'll see what the future holds, Dar Dar'.

DAR DAR: 'We will. There's a lot to take in there but I'm speechless. People are going to be talking about him'.

TONY: 'They will be. I'll see you later buddy'.